CAMARO

Michael Bradley

mc **Marshall Cavendish**
Benchmark
New York

Marshall Cavendish Benchmark
99 White Plains Road
Tarrytown, NY 10591
www.marshallcavendish.us

All websites were available and accurate when this book was sent to press.

Library of Congress Cataloging-in-Publication Data

Bradley, Michael, 1962—
Camaro / by Michael Bradley.
    p. cm. — (Cars)
Includes index.
ISBN 978-0-7614-4104-5
 1. Camaro automobile—Juvenile literature. I.Title.
TL215.C6B73 2010
629.222'2—dc22
2008027817

Editor: Megan Comerford
Publisher: Michelle Bisson
Art Director: Anahid Hamparian
Series designer: Daniel Roode

Photo research by Connie Gardner

Cover photo by Ron Kimball/www.kimballstock.com

The photographs in this book are used by permission and through the courtesy of:
Ron Kimball/www.kimballstock.com: back cover, 1, 7, 8, 16, 18, 20, 25, 29; *Corbis*: Steve Fecht, 4; Tom Pidgeon, 6; Kevin Christopher Ou, 10; Transtock, 12; Bettmann, 19; Car Culture, 23; *Alamy*: Stan Rohrer, 13; *Getty Images*: Car Culture, 14; *GM Media Archive*: 15, 21, 24, 27, 28; *AP Photos*: Jennifer Graylock, 26.

Printed in Malaysia
1 3 5 6 4 2

CONTENTS

Chevrolet let late-night talk-show host Jay Leno drive their 2009 concept car to a classic car show in California.

Most Americans know Jay Leno as a comedian and the host of the popular late-night program *The Tonight Show*. On a warm July evening in 2006, he was more than that—and he loved it. Leno is a funny man, to be sure, but he's also a car nut. His three garages house more than fifty cars and as many motorcycles, all classics.

So he was right at home driving a 2009 Chevrolet Camaro into the parking lot of the Bob's Big Boy restaurant in Burbank, California. For once, the TV star wasn't the reason people were pointing and talking. They were surprised to see him, but they were just as impressed with the Camaro, which had been part of America's automotive muscle club for thirty-five years. It was making a return to the American road, and it was doing so in grand style.

The Chevrolet Camaro concept takes a spin down the runway at the International Auto Show in Detroit as photographers crowd the stage to snap photos of the new car.

The sleek, powerful machine was still almost two years from a full comeback, but there had been hints. At the 2006 International Auto Show in Detroit, Michigan, Chevrolet introduced a concept Camaro. There were no formal plans to produce the car, but the **enthusiastic response** of drivers and auto writers led Chevy to announce seven months later that the Camaro was indeed coming back for 2009. The next year, a smoking-hot orange Camaro convertible was the hit of the auto show. It even **overshadowed** a crowd of celebrities Chevy invited to join the **festivities**. Carmen Electra, Nick Lachey, Jennifer Hudson, Nick Cannon, Kristen Bell, and Minka Kelly all looked good. But the Camaro looked better.

No offense to the stars, but since its introduction in late 1966, the Camaro has been one of America's most impressive rides. Although it was often compared to the Ford Mustang, the Camaro was able to develop its own personality over the years. Even though it was retired in 2002, few could ever question the Camaro's performance. It was a

Camaros are great-looking cars, and some owners like to customize theirs with souped-up engines or special paint jobs. This 1968 Camaro features a metallic blue hood and flame detailing.

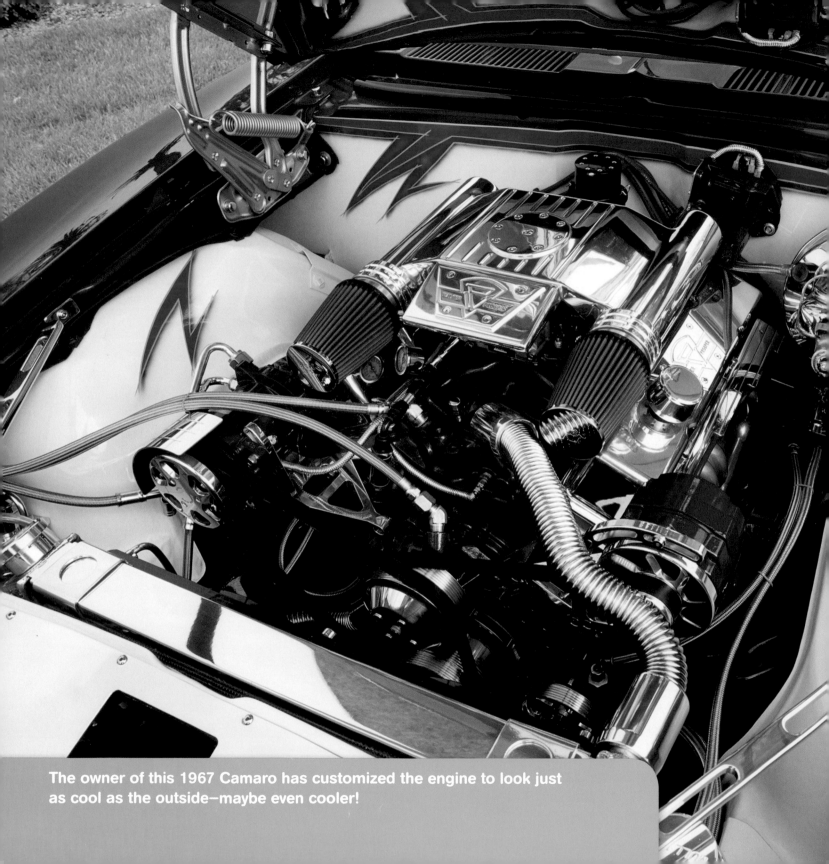

The owner of this 1967 Camaro has customized the engine to look just as cool as the outside—maybe even cooler!

true power hitter and it looked every bit the part of a strongman, from the moment it hit **showrooms** until Chevy's decision to stop its production.

The Camaro was low to the ground and powered by a **growling** V-8 engine that made it faster than just about any other car on the scene. Over the years, it changed to keep up with new rules and regulations, but the Camaro was always at heart a sports car that longed to crank it up on an open road. Chevy never took away the Camaro's spirit. The car continued to **outperform** the competition, even when it had to improve its gas **mileage** and become friendlier to the environment. Through all the changes, the Camaro's personality stayed the same.

When Leno drove that new Camaro into the parking lot, the cameras were running and the crowd was excited. People could hear the rumble of the motor and see the sleek design of the new car. The Camaro was back, and it looked to be better than ever—if that was possible.

Chevrolet hoped that their 1968 Corvair Monza would be a big success. But, with poor gas mileage and rumors that the sports car was unsafe, Chevy was forced to stop production.

CHAPTER TWO
A WORTHY CHALLENGER

Blame Ralph Nader. Or, if you want, give him credit. If the man who fought for **consumer** rights for decades hadn't written a book in 1965, we might be celebrating the Corvair right now. But Nader took direct aim at that Chevy sports car in his book, *Unsafe at Any Speed: The Designed-In Dangers of the American Sports Car.*

Okay, so the book wasn't all about the Corvair, but the first chapter was. It described the car's safety **flaws** and explained how its drivers and passengers were at risk. Nader was right, and the next seven chapters talked about plenty of other cars. No other, however, had its own section. Chevy made the necessary changes to the Corvair, but the damage was done.

The Corvair was a pretty sharp car, so car enthusiasts were sad to see it go. In fact, the 1961 Monza model

This 1967 Camaro Rally Sport (RS) was one of the first models.

was called "the poor man's Porsche" by some critics, because of its European styling. Ford thought so much of it that it created the Mustang as a response. And what a response.

In one year, Ford sold more than 400,000 of its new sports car, making the Mustang the best-selling new car in history. The Corvair was in big trouble, and so was Chevy. Even though Chevrolet **redesigned** the Corvair, it didn't matter. Something new was needed.

Though some in the company believed it could challenge the Mustang with the Nova, the Chevelle, or the Corvette, they were wrong. So, a top-secret program was started to design a new car. It was code-named "F Body" within the company, and called "Panther" in the automotive press. It featured engineering and design that were different from other Chevy models. However, because it was supposed to be an answer to the Mustang, the car couldn't be *too* different. That's why some say Chevy stole the idea for the Camaro from Ford. Others don't care about that. They just like the car.

Chevrolet installed a special V-8 engine in all its 1969 Camaro Z28s. It was built for speed and could accelerate from 0 to 60 miles per hour (0 to 96.5 km/h) in just 7.4 seconds!

Those fans had a lot of company on September 29, 1966, when the Camaro hit the showrooms. Its name, which wasn't announced until earlier that month, came from a 1935 French-English dictionary and meant "friend" or "comrade." The Camaro came in two **versions**, a coupe and a convertible, and sold for $2,466. Those who wanted a little more style could **upgrade** to the Rally Sport (RS) or Super Sport (SS) model. They were lower to the ground and more powerful than Mustang. When editors at *Motor Trend*, the country's top automotive magazine, saw the Camaro, they put the car on the cover.

The Camaro is just as much an icon of the 1960s America as White Castle. Sales really began to take off in 1968 with models like this Camaro 396 hardtop coupe.

The Indianapolis 500 selected the Camaro as its pace car in 1967—the first year the car was in production!

The Camaro was wide, so it handled well on sharp turns and wet roads. It was a rounder, smoother car than the Mustang, and buyers could choose from three different V-8 engines. That December, drivers who wanted some serious power could try the Z28, a Camaro with a powerful 290-**horsepower** engine and some nice exterior trim. The Camaro had arrived with a bang, helping to begin the muscle-car era with a strong response to Ford. The following May, it was the official **pace car** for the **Indianapolis 500**, only the third Chevy model to hold that honor. Instead of crumbling after the attack on the Corvair, Chevy delivered a strong counterpunch.

The Camaro was on the roads, and Chevrolet was back in business.

This 1968 Camaro Prostreet was designed for drag racing. As if the orange body with purple stripes isn't enough, the car has a blower on the hood that helps cool the engine.

The Camaro had made a big splash. Now came the hard part: trying to keep it going. Chevy believed the best way to do that was to make the car more powerful. The late 1960s were the height of the muscle-car movement, and the Camaro was a big part of it.

The 1968 Camaros were all about power, performance, and driving fun. Americans no longer wanted just family sedans and station wagons. They wanted excitement, too. So, Chevy gave it to them. The Z28 was so powerful, it went from 0 to 60 miles per hour (mph) (0 to 96.5 kilometers per hour) in a cheetah-like 5.3 seconds. For some, it wasn't enough. A dealer in western Pennsylvania put a giant

The 1970 Camaro was longer, wider, and lower to the ground than earlier versions of the car. This Hugger Orange RS/SS model has round front parking lights and a black grille.

427-cubic-inch (7 liter) engine into a Camaro and reached 183 mph (295 km/h). Others did the same thing, turning the car into their own laboratories and creating versions that were even more muscular.

Proof of the car's popularity came the following year, 1969, when Chevy sold 243,085 Camaros. That model was called "The Hugger," because it was so low to the ground that it appeared to be grabbing, or hugging, the road. The folks at the Indy 500 liked it, too, and made the Camaro the official pace car for the second time in three years. The launch had been successful. The Camaro had arrived.

And just like that, it was time to redesign. The first generation Camaro was a response to Mustang, and in many ways it looked like the Ford model. In 1970, Chevrolet looked to Europe for **inspiration**, basing the Camaro on the Ferraris of the 1960s rather than the Mustang. The result was a wider car that looked more like a European sedan but could still kick it out on the open road.

Race-car drivers Bobby Unser (12) and A. J. Foyt (10) drove identical Camaros in the 1975 International Race of Champions. Unser eventually pulled ahead to win the race—but only by about 12 inches!

Trouble was, America wasn't looking for power any more. Some people and businesses thought that muscle-car owners took too many chances on the road. Meanwhile, the government was forcing auto-makers to produce cars that were better for the environment and used less gas. The early 1970s were tough for the Camaro as sales fell. But by the end of the decade things were looking up, for a couple reasons. The first had its roots in a 1974 decision by **legendary** race-car driver Roger Penske and Riverside International Raceway president Les Richter to develop the International Race of Champions. They chose the Z28 as the car for the race, and that helped boost sales of the Camaro.

In 1979 Chevrolet set a sales record for its Camaro Z28. The model had side vents and "Z28" painted in bold letters on the doors.

The third-generation Camaro Z28s look very different from models introduced before 1982. Changes included square headlights and a smoother body.

By the end of the decade, sales had gone up, especially for the Z28. The Camaro had its best year ever in 1979, when more than 282,000 were sold. But Chevy still wanted more from the Camaro. The Pontiac Trans Am had become a popular competitor, and the Mustang was still selling well. As early as 1975, Chevrolet knew it needed some help, so it began designing its third generation of Camaros, hoping for a 1980 debut.

The new generation model didn't show up until 1982, but it was worth the wait. It looked like a 1960s-era car and was extremely popular. Sales rose steadily until 1984, thanks to the car's style, performance, and good gas mileage. It was a high point, but it wouldn't last. Storm clouds were on the horizon that would threaten the Camaro's future. The next two decades were tough and would bring an end to the car—and a new beginning.

Silver anniversaries are usually occasions for celebration, especially in the car industry. Any model that lasts twenty-five years has to have something special, something worth recognizing.

But when the Camaro turned twenty-five in 1992, people were worried. Sales of the model had sagged. The Z28, the Camaro's symbol of power and muscle, had been **abandoned** and then brought back. Dodge had taken over as the official International Race of Champions car. Things weren't looking good.

It was a risky environment for a relaunch, but in 1993 the Camaro was back with a new look and style.

The 1992 Camaro Z28 convertible marked the twenty-fifth production year for the car. There were fewer than 1,300 produced, and each cost over $21,000.

Chevy could have made it a front-wheel-drive car, just like almost everything else on American roads. It could have taken away its spirit and made it a four-cylinder, fuel-efficient model. That didn't happen. The Generation IV Camaro was another performance car, with a standard V-6. It came in two versions, the Sport Coupe and the Z28. And it was fast.

It was fast enough that the Indianapolis 500 wanted it again. For the fourth time, the Camaro was the Indy 500's Official Pace Car. Anybody who drove it was impressed with its performance. It was faster and stronger than the Mustang. But once again, the Mustang

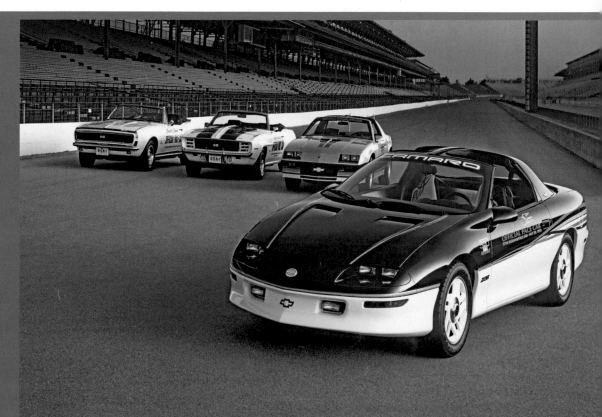

The Camaro was the first car to be selected as the Indianapolis 500 pace car four times: 1967, 1969, 1982, and 1993. The 1993 Z28 pace car was a T-top painted black and white with special decals.

The Camaro celebrated its thirtieth anniversary in 1997 with a white Camaro SS with orange racing stripes. It looked like a sleek, modern version of the 1969 pace car.

outsold the Camaro, this time by a two-to-one margin. Real drivers knew how good the Camaro was. People who only cared about looks favored the Mustang's **retro** styling.

But Chevrolet kept trying. In 1994 the Camaro convertible reappeared. Chevy teamed with various specialty shops to create performance models that had even more power. In 1998 the company even imported Jim Perkins, a Toyota design executive, to take a crack at the car. He made big changes that turned the Camaro into a sharp sedan. But it wasn't a muscle car. Sales were low and falling. When the Mustang introduced its new look in 1999, the Camaro was in big trouble. Even though it won every performance test against the Ford model, the Camaro couldn't win where it counted: in the sales war.

Chevy made no noticeable changes in the Camaro between 1999 and 2002. Sales continued to drop. The end was near. On September 26, 2001, Chevy made it official: The Camaro was going out of production. By 2003, it was gone.

Or was it? Two years later, engineers began working on a new Camaro **concept car**. It was low and wide, just like the original. And it was powerful—really powerful. No more sacrificing muscle for looks. In fact, at 400 horsepower, the new V-8 Camaro would have strength to

A bright orange concept Camaro convertible with black racing stripes was on display at the 2007 New York International Auto Show.

Chevrolet workers sculpt a full-size model of the new Camaro, set to hit the roads in 2009.

overpower any stretch of road and the sharp styling that would make just about anybody take notice.

On January 8, 2006, Chevy introduced the Camaro to the world at the International Auto Show in Detroit. The response was **overwhelming**. People flocked to the exhibit to see the silver bullet. And they all had one question: Will Chevrolet build it? They had their answer in August. Yes, the new 2010 Camaro would be available in 2009. A year later, Chevy unveiled the bright orange convertible at the auto show. TV, music, and movie stars surrounded it, but none could match the Camaro for true star power. Just five years earlier, the car was dead and buried. Now, the whole world could see that the Camaro was back.

And ready to roar.

Vital Statistics

1967 Camaro Z28

Power: 290 hp
Engine Size: 302 ci/4.9L
Engine Type: Small block 302 V-8
Weight: 3,500 lbs (1,588 kg)
Top Speed: 140 mph (225 km/h)
0–60 mph (0–96.5 km/h): 6.9 sec

2010 Camaro Coupe

Power: 300 hp
Engine Size: 220 ci/3.6L
Engine Type: LLT V-6
Weight: 3,760 lbs (1,706 kg)
Top Speed: 155 mph (249 km/h)
0–60 mph (0–96.5 km/h): 6.1 sec

GLOSSARY

abandon   To leave or give up on something with no plans to return.

concept car   A car made to show off a new idea, style, or technology, often first shown at car shows.

consumer   A person who buys goods and services for his or her own use.

enthusiastic   Having or showing intense interest or desire.

festivities   Celebrations or parties.

flaws   Mistakes or errors.

growling   Making a low, rumbling sound, like thunder.

horsepower   The unit used to measure an engine's power. The more horsepower (hp), the stronger the engine and the faster a car can travel.

Indianapolis 500   America's most famous auto race, which is run in Indianapolis, Indiana, every Memorial Day weekend.

inspiration   Something that gives someone an idea.

legendary   Famous.

mileage   The average number of miles a vehicle can travel using one gallon of gasoline.

outperform   To perform better than a competitor.

overshadow   To be more important than something else.

overwhelm   To overpower.

pace car   A car that leads the competing cars through a warm-up lap, but does not take part in the race.

redesign   To create a new look or improved function for an old model, such as a car.

response	An answer or reply.
retro	Using styles or fashions that were popular in the past.
showroom	The part of an automotive dealership where new cars are displayed for customers to look at them.
upgrade	To make something better by adding to it or changing a part or parts of it.
version	One form of a product or idea.

FURTHER INFORMATION

BOOKS

Gunnell, John, and Jerry Heasley. *The Story of Camaro*. Iola, WI: Krause Publications, 2006.

Holmstrom, Darwin. *Camaro: Forty Years*. St. Paul, MN: Motorbooks, 2007.

Young, Anthony. *Camaro*. St. Paul, MN: Motorbooks, 2004.

WEBSITES

www.chevrolet.com/camaro/

www.camaroz28.com

www.edmunds.com/chevrolet/camaro/history.html

Page numbers in **boldface** are photographs.

About the Author

MICHAEL BRADLEY is a writer and broadcaster who lives near Philadelphia. He has written for *Sports Illustrated for Kids, Hoop, Inside Stuff,* and *Slam* magazines and is a regular contributor to Comcast SportsNet in Philadelphia.